I. T. Hecker

The Catholic Church in the United States

Its rise, relations with the republic, growth, and future prospects

I. T. Hecker

The Catholic Church in the United States
Its rise, relations with the republic, growth, and future prospects

ISBN/EAN: 9783744646635

Printed in Europe, USA, Canada, Australia, Japan

Cover: Foto ©Lupo / pixelio.de

More available books at **www.hansebooks.com**

THE

CATHOLIC CHURCH

IN THE

UNITED STATES.

ITS RISE, RELATIONS WITH THE REPUBLIC,

GROWTH, AND FUTURE PROSPECTS.

BY

REV. I. T. HECKER.

―――――

NEW YORK:
THE CATHOLIC PUBLICATION SOCIETY CO.
9 Barclay Street.

1879.

THE NATION PRESS, 27 ROSE STREET, NEW YORK.

[From THE CATHOLIC WORLD for July, 1879.]

THE CATHOLIC CHURCH

IN THE

UNITED STATES.*

———•———

WE propose in the following pages to treat of the original elements of the Catholic Church in the United States, her relations with the republic, the causes of her growth, and her future prospects.

The discovery of the western continent was eminently a religious enterprise. Columbus had in vain sought aid for his great undertaking from his native city, Genoa, from Portugal, England, Venice, and the court of Spain; and it was after these fruitless applications that Juan Perez, the prior of La Rabida, took up his cause and pleaded it with so much earnestness and ability in a letter to Queen Isabella that she at once sent for Columbus and offered to pledge her jewels to obtain funds for the expedition. The motive which animated Columbus, in common with the Franciscan prior and Isabella the Catholic, was the burning desire to carry the blessings of the Christian faith to the inhabitants of a new continent, and it was the inspiration of this idea which brought a new world to light.

This inspiration has never died out; if the Spanish and French missionaries did not accompany the first discoverers, they followed speedily in their tracks, and the work of the conversion of the aborigines was earnestly begun. In a short time they traversed the whole northern continent from the mouth of the St. Lawrence to California, and from the Gulf of Mexico to Hudson's Bay. Sometimes missionaries were slain, but the fearless soldiers of the cross continued unceasingly their work of converting the natives and bringing them into the fold of Christ. Though the pages of history which narrate the self-sacrificing labors of the missionaries to the Indians are among the brightest in the annals of the church; still the whole number of Catholic Indians will not appear as a large item in the sum of her members in the United States. One of the reasons for this is that the heroic efforts made for their conversion and civilization have been in a great measure thwarted by the inhuman pol-

* Bancroft's *History of the United States.*
"The Catholic Peril in America." By Francis E Abbott. *The Fortnightly Review,* March, 1876.
The Papacy and the Civil Power. By R. W. Thompson.
Future of the Republic. By Ralph Waldo Emerson.
Democracy in Europe: a History. By Sir Thomas Erskine May.
Romanism and High Schools. By the Rev. Joseph Cook. A lecture delivered in Tremont Temple, Boston, March 17, 1879.

icy pursued towards the Indians. Yet, when we come to consider the actual elements which blend together in forming the Catholic Church in the republic of the United States, her faithful children of the forests ought not to be left out of the count. According to the report of the Bureau of Indian Affairs for 1875 the whole number of Indians under the government of the United States is about 279,333, and it is estimated, on good authority, that of these 106,000 are Catholics.

The raising of the red men to the height of the Christian faith was but one of the fruits of the discovery of the new continent; another was to offer an asylum to all who in other lands were persecuted and oppressed on account of their religious convictions. Among the first to seek this relief from oppression on the virgin soil of the New World were the English Catholic colonists under Lord Baltimore. To their honor it is to be said that, both by the original design of the proprietary, Lord Baltimore, and by the legislative enactments of the freemen of the province, there reigned, while their rule lasted in Maryland, a perfect equality among all Christian denominations, and to all were secured the same rights and privileges, civil and religious. This act on the part of the colonists of Maryland was in harmony with the dictates of right reason and the authentic teachings of faith; for all attempts to bring by coercion men who differ in their religious convictions to uniformity in the profession of religious belief, if successful, would logically put an end to all rational religion. Compulsion never gave birth to faith, which is "not by any means a blind assent of the mind," * but

* Vatican Council, De Fide, ch. iii.

essentially an intelligent and voluntary act. Convinced of this, as Catholics, the idea of religious tolerance flowed naturally and consistently in the minds of the first settlers on the shores of the Potomac. It was a noble act on their part to proclaim that within the province and jurisdiction of Maryland no Christian man should be molested in worshipping God according to the dictates of his conscience, and whoever supposes that the Syllabus teaches anything to the contrary seriously mistakes its meaning. Honor, then, to the pilgrim fathers of St. Mary! who, when the other settlements had a state-supported church and were intolerant to all others, asked for themselves no favor, but offered equal rights to all; thus excluding the secular authority of the state from interfering in matters of religion—a principle for which the popes, in their struggles with the secular powers for the rights of the church, have always contended, and for which they still have to contend. Let, then, those Catholic Anglo-Americans have their due share of praise for the religious toleration of which they were the first to give an example—an example, furthermore, which had a formative influence in shaping the republic and its free institutions. For the principle of the incompetency of the state to enact laws controlling matters purely religious is the keystone of the arch of American liberties, and Catholics of all climes can point to it with special delight. This noble course of the Catholics of Maryland, however, was little appreciated, and they were hindered in their progress and trampled upon when those to whom they had so generously offered a refuge from persecution had attained to power in the province;

nevertheless, they kept their faith, and were by far the largest part of the body of the Catholic Church up to the time when the great tide of immigration set in towards the shores of the United States, and their descendants still form a prominent and influential portion of the Catholic community.

The next original element was that furnished by France. The soil of the United States was at an early period watered by the blood of the French missionaries to the Indian tribes. In 1775 an accession to the church came through the expulsion by the Puritans of Massachusetts of a colony of French Catholics from Acadia, on the Bay of Fundy. In spite of the solemn engagements of the capitulation, that they should not be disturbed, they were driven from their peaceful homes, and about seven thousand were scattered among the British colonies. These are the Acadians whose sad tale has been told by Longfellow in the beautiful poem of *Evangeline.* The influence exerted by the flower of the French army and nobility who entered the service of the infant republic at a time when, but for their aid, its cause would likely have been lost, in removing prejudices from the minds of colonists against the Catholic religion, and compelling them to show at least a decent respect for the religious convictions of their Catholic allies, is not lightly to be estimated. Then the storm of the French Revolution drove to the shores of the United States, between the years 1791 and 1799, a body of apostolic clergymen whose labors reanimated the zeal of Catholics, caused conversions to the faith, organized new parishes, founded seminaries and colleges, and created bishoprics. It would be difficult to estimate the influence which these French missionaries exercised throughout the country by their exemplary lives, their learning, their virtues, and their qualities as men. Among them was a Maréchal, a Cheverus, a Bruté, a Flaget, and a Dubois. Twenty-three French priests came at that period to aid the young church in the United States; six were made bishops, and of these Maréchal became the third archbishop of Baltimore. Cheverus was the first bishop of Boston, and was recalled to France and made archbishop of Bordeaux and cardinal.

To these are to be added several thousand Catholics, among whom were some hundred colored people who came from San Domingo and other West Indian islands in 1793 to escape the effects of the French Revolution and the negro insurrection. These French Catholics added faith, piety, wealth to the infant church, and their posterity, constant to their religion, rank among the distinguished citizens of the republic. Their number was also considerably increased by the territories acquired or admitted to the Union, which were mostly inhabited by French Catholics. Louisiana was acquired in 1803, and had at that time about thirty-two thousand inhabitants, nearly all of whom were Catholics. Besides these were other settlements, peopled by the descendants mostly of French-Canadians, at St. Louis, Detroit, Vincennes, which have grown since into places of importance, and still retain the deep imprint of the French race.

Moreover, the immigration of the French from Canada to the United States has been slowly on the increase, and in recent years has grown rapidly in volume. On inquiry made of a dignitary of one of the principal dioceses of Canada, we were told that the number of French-Canadians who had emigrated to the United States during a period of thirty years should be estimated at five hundred thousand. The presence of this Canadian element is a marked feature in all the dioceses bordering on Canada, which contain a considerable number of parishes composed entirely of French-Canadians. Thus it will be seen that the Catholic French element was an active and important one, both in regard to character and numbers, in the formation of the Catholic Church in the New World.

The Catholics from Ireland will not be found so numerous as those from England and France among the early settlers of North America. The Irish settlers, however considerable their aggregate number may have been, were not concentrated in any one locality like the Spanish, French, or English. A number of Catholic Irishmen, however, or their descendants, one of whom was Charles Carroll, the signer of the Declaration of Independence, took an active part in the struggle for independence. The first commodore, the father of the American navy, was John Barry, born in Ireland, a faithful Catholic, a true American, and an able seaman. But before the great exodus Ireland had given to America prelates distinguished for their faith, virtue, learning, eloquence, and apostolic zeal—prelates such as Bishop England, Archbishops Kenrick and Hughes. No man did more in his day than Bishop England to make the Catholic Church respected. Love for the free institutions of his adopted country was with him a vital prin-

ciple, and often prompted his eloquence. Bishop England as a pulpit orator was unrivalled, and may be called the Chrysostom of the American Church. The first bishop and archbishop of the church in the United States, John Carroll, and the first in North America to be invested with the dignity of the cardinalate, the Archbishop of New York, John McCloskey, were Irishmen by descent.

But the famine of 1846–1847 gave the impetus to a mighty stream of immigration which did not cease in volume until it supplied millions of faithful children to the young church in America and rapidly extended her borders. The number of immigrants from Ireland who arrived at the port of New York during the thirty years ending in 1876 was 2,001,727.

There will not be found in the Catholic Church in the United States a people, as a class, more devoted, sincere, and better instructed in their religion than the Germans. The number of their churches, schools, seminaries, hospitals, orphan asylums will compare advantageously, from an intellectual no less than a material point of view, with those of any other portion of the Catholic population. None are better supplied with priests for their people and teachers for their children than the Germans. The religious orders flourish among them, and are represented by the Benedictines, with several abbots; the Capuchins, and other branches of the order of St. Francis; the Jesuits, Redemptorists, and other religious congregations both of men and of women, especially such as are devoted to teaching. In the hierarchy there is one German archbishop, and a considerable number of the bishops are German by birth or descent. The Catholic German element had been almost insignificant until the period including the last thirty years; for although Catholics are considerably in the majority in South Germany, immigration to the United States in the past was mostly from the Protestant states. According to the latest and most accurate computation of German Catholics in the United States, they number 1,237,563 souls.

Conversions to the Catholic faith during the early part of the century were few and isolated instances; but within the last twenty-five years they have become more numerous. Speaking on this subject, a French writer who visited, twelve or more years ago, the United States, says: "It is difficult to apply a statistical table to the study of the question of conversions. The different Protestant sects furnish very unequal contingents to the little army of souls daily returning to the true faith; and it is a curious fact that the two sects which furnish the most are the Episcopalians, who in their forms and traditions approach nearest to the Catholic Church, and the Unitarians, who go to the very opposite extreme, and appear to push their philosophical and rationalistic principles almost beyond the pale of Christianity. These two sects generally comprise the most enlightened and intellectual people of North America." *

This observation is exact and has a profound reason for its basis. The human mind is uneasy until it has reached unity and grasps universal truth. And this is arrived at by two diverse but equally legitimate ways. Those who are born in sectarianism, as soon as

* E. Rameau, *Le Correspondant*, 1865.

they allow their reason to act on their faith learn that they have but fragments of Christian truth; and by tracing these to their logical connection with other truths contained in divine revelation they gain by degrees the knowledge of the whole body of revealed truth. Having reached this stage of preparation, there breaks upon their mental vision the divine character and mission of the Catholic Church. This once seen, to enter her fold becomes a test both of their intellectual consistency and of the sincerity of their faith in Christianity. This is the road which leads Episcopalians and others who still retain firmly one or more of the revealed truths of Christianity to the Catholic Church. The second class fall back upon the essential truths of natural reason. This basis recovered, the rejection of sectarianism logically follows, for the denial of any one truth of divine revelation involves of necessity a contradiction of human reason. Indignant at this, they ask rightly for a religion which is consonant with the dictates of reason and finds its foundation in the human breast. Americans who have repudiated Protestantism on the grounds of reason—and they are not a few—have made the discovery that the exposition of Christianity by the Catholic Church agrees with the dictates of reason and that it takes in its scope all the faculties of human nature. This is the Unitarian road, which is destined, in our opinion, to become the great American highway to the Catholic Church.

There is scarcely an American family, distinguished either by its ancestry, or by its social position, or by its wealth, which to-day has not one or more representatives among the converts to the Catholic Church. In some parts of the country there are congregations almost altogether made up of converts. Converts will be found among the archbishops, bishops, and clergy, and a fair share also belong to the different learned professions or hold positions of similar respectability. Statistics which bear upon this point vary. In some dioceses the number of converts among the confirmed is as high as twelve per cent., in others it is about seven per cent., and in others again not more than five, while elsewhere probably the proportion is smaller. To the foregoing source of Catholic increase is to be added the accession of Florida by purchase in 1819, containing a population of about 18,000; also the acquisition of Texas in 1845, and California and New Mexico in 1848, having about 160,000 inhabitants. These people were for the most part of Spanish-American blood, and nearly all Catholics. Finally, if we add from a rough guess 25,000 to 30,000 colored people, we have all the original elements which the power of the Catholic faith has blended together in one, forming the organization and strength of the Catholic Church in the republic of the United States.

The connection between the republic and the Catholic Church, if satisfactorily treated, requires that the fundamental principles of the republic should be clearly stated, and their relation with Protestantism first be disposed of. This is what we now attempt.

The republic of the United States is the result of the gathered political wisdom and experience of past ages, shaped by a recognition of man's natural rights and a trust in his innate capacity for self-government beyond what had found expression in the prevailing political systems of Europe. The fundamental articles of the American political creed and the formative principles of the republic are embodied in the Declaration of Independence, whence they passed gradually into the constitutions of the several States and into the Constitution of the United States, and have step by step worked their way more or less perfectly into the general and special laws of the country. These articles consist principally in the declaration " that all men are created equal; that they are endowed by their Creator with certain inalienable rights; that among these are life, liberty, and the pursuit of happiness; that, to secure these rights, governments are instituted among men, deriving their just powers from the consent of the governed."

These declarations can be looked upon only by superficial thinkers as "glittering generalities," whereas some are divine and fundamental, and all are practical verities, having a ground both in reason and revelation. They are divine, inasmuch as they declare the rights of the Creator in his creature; they are fundamental, for without the enjoyment of the natural rights which they proclaim man is not a man, but a slave or a chattel; they are practical, for man is, or ought to be, under his Creator, the master of his own destiny and free from any dominion not founded in divine right. The Creator invested man with these rights in order that he might fulfil the duties inseparably attached to them. For these rights put man in the possession of himself, and leave him free to reach the end for which his Creator called him into existence. He, therefore, who denies or violates these rights offends God, acts the tyrant, and is an enemy of mankind. And if there be any superior merit in the republican polity of the United States, it consists chiefly in this: that while it adds nothing and can add nothing to man's natural rights, it exp esses more clearly, guards more securely, and protects more effectually these rights ; so that man, under its popular institutions, enjoys greater liberty in working out his true destiny.

Since Christianity claims to be God's revelation of the great end for which he created man, it follows that those rights without which he cannot reach that end must find their sanction, expressed or implied, in all true interpretations of its doctrines.

That the interpretations of Christianity by the so-called Reformation, especially by its leaders, neither sanctioned nor even implied the natural rights of man, the peculiar articles of its creed and its history plainly show.

When the Puritan Fathers landed on Plymouth Rock they brought with them a fixed religious creed, whose primary article was "the total depravity " of human nature, and, as a consequence, the loss of free-will ; from which premise it was held that man, in his unregenerate state, is not able to do any good, but is inclined to all evil. This fundamental dogma, applied to the political order, excludes unregenerate men from all part in the organization of the state, as well as from all participation in the rights and privileges of citizenship. Such, too, is the historical fact ; political citizenship in the province of the Puritans, where they trim-

med the state to suit their creed, was exclusively granted to members of the orthodox church. " All civil power," says the Presbyterian Dr. Hodge, " was confined to the members of the church, no person being either eligible to office or entitled to the right of suffrage who was not in full communion of some church."[*] The natural man had no rights. To be a freeman you must be a Puritan. The men who came in the *Mayflower* did not hold the principles which gave birth to religious toleration or political liberty in the New World. And so far were their annals from the " grand historic lines of the country " that it was as late as 1834 when Massachusetts granted full religious liberty, while even to-day a Catholic is ineligible to office in the State of New Hampshire because of his religion. Hence there can scarcely be an assertion farther from the truth than that made by Ranke and D'Aubigné, and repeated by Bancroft and men of less or more note, that republican liberty is due to Protestantism, and due to Protestantism under its most repulsive form—that which was given to it by John Calvin.

An appeal to the New World, where the original Protestant colonies were free to form a political government in accordance with their peculiar religious belief, gives no countenance to this peremptory assertion. It is, moreover, made in face of the historic testimony of the Old World, for nowhere in Europe has Protestantism been favorable to popular rights, or called into existence what by any honest interpretation can be termed a republic. This statement can be easily verified. During its three centuries of existence a republican form of government has nowhere under Protestant ascendency made its appearance. One will look in vain in Germany, the cradle of Protestantism, for a popular government. The same is true of Prussia, England, Scotland, Sweden, and Holland, for the Dutch Republic was founded upon the ancient constitutions of the provinces, and not upon popular rights. It was a republic only in name, and, such as it was, its life was very short. M. Guizot, in his *Life of John Calvin*, reveals the cause for this, and rightly discriminates between the influence of Calvinism on churches and the influence of Calvinism on liberty when he says: "Calvin's *Institutes* were the source of the strength and vitality of the Reformed churches in these countries," but at the same time he acknowledges that "their claims were incompatible with the progress of liberty" (Guizot's *Life of John Calvin*, ch. v.) "Calvin did not believe in man's free-will," says the same author, "and he treated it with severity and a kind of contempt. Calvin believed and asserted that he had more right over other men's opinions and actions than he ought to have claimed, and he did not show sufficient respect for their rights" (*ibid.*) He knows little of the origin of liberty in America or elsewhere who honors in any sense John Calvin as its author.

If Protestants have contributed to human freedom, it was not as Protestants; the motives which prompted them did not spring from their religious creed, for that was a foe to human rights and the grave of liberty. The servitude of the human will in consequence of original sin, as taught by both Martin Luther and John Calvin, cut off,

root and branch, personal, political, civil, intellectual, moral, and religious liberty. Protestantism as a religious system was an insult to all ideas of freedom. Hence it was not due to any principle of liberty of the original Protestant colonists that religious toleration was made a part of the organic law of the republic, but to the fact that the Protestant sects were not able to agree, and that there was no one of them sufficiently powerful to press its exclusive claim and get its peculiarities incorporated into the Constitution.

In no place where Protestantism prevailed among a people as their religion has it given birth to a republic, and nowhere in the nineteenth century does there exist a republic in a Protestant land. The so-called Reformation, following out its own principles, failed altogether to reconcile Christianity with popular rights. Its spirit and doctrines, derived from an exaggerated idea of the sovereignty of God and the utter nullity of man, are in accordance with the Oriental mind and suitable to an Asiatic despotism, and it deserves credit for civil and religious liberty nowhere. As for the Puritans in particular, one of their descendants covers the whole ground when he says: "I believe we are descended from the Puritans, who nobly fled from a land of despotism to a land of freedom, where they could not only enjoy their own religion but prevent everybody else from enjoying his."

Protestantism in its political aspect might be defined as a theocratic corporation composed exclusively of regenerate men of orthodox faith, having for its premise the religious dogma concerning the "total corruption of human nature" in consequence of Adam's fall, as taught by its leaders, Martin Luther and John Calvin. One may repel this conclusion, but it will be at the expense of intellectual consistency and historical testimony.

So long as the New England settlements were content to remain English colonies it was possible for them to hold their peculiar religious tenets and maintain their exclusive religio-political organization; but when they joined with the other colonies, and appealed to the equality by birth of all men and the inalienable rights of man to justify their separation from Great Britain, the Puritans then and there, in sanctioning these declarations, entered upon a road which necessarily terminated in a radical and total change of the peculiar articles of their religious creed. For the proclamation of man's natural rights involved the overthrow of the whole theological structure built by the reformed theologians upon the corner-stone of man's "total depravity." The Puritans, in signing the Declaration of Independence, signed their own death-warrant.

A comparison between the two will show this. The political system of the Puritans was founded on an exaggerated supernaturalism; the political system implied in the truths contained in the Declaration of Independence supposed a mere naturalism. The former held human nature to be totally corrupt; the latter supposes human nature as essentially good. The one maintained that man, by Adam's fall, forfeited all his natural rights; the other declared that the rights of man by nature are inalienable. The first granted political suffrage exclusively to the elect; the second based the right of suffrage on universal manhood. The Puritans relied altogether on the strength of divine grace; the American republican trusted in the inborn capacity of human nature. The two parties started from opposite poles in regard to man's rights and the value of human nature. The Declaration of Independence was the antithesis of Martin Luther's work on the *Slave-will* and John Calvin's *Institutes*, looked at from their political side.

That Calvinism excludes republicanism in politics has been shown; and that republicanism excludes Calvinism in religion we will now endeavor to prove.

The process of this exclusion was a simple one. The natural influence of the practical working of the American political system, based on universal suffrage, is an incitement to the intelligence and conscience of the people under the conviction that the choice of the ballot-box will be in the main on the side of good government. Frequent elections and the popular agitations attending them awaken aspirations, excite debate and action, and under this stimulating influence the people are soon led to trust human reason and to become conscious of the possession of freewill; and it was quite natural that, as these repressed powers grew in strength by action, their leaders should assert, and rather defiantly at first, the rights of man, be forward as champions of human liberty, and indulge in some pretty "tall talk" about the dignity of man and the nobility of human nature. Nor can it be a matter of surprise that rousing appeals were made to men who, under the depressing influence of a religious creed, would have lost their manhood, if that were possible: "to

act out your self," "obey your instincts," "assert your manhood,"
"be a man"! The extravagant efforts to magnify man were the natural rebound from the opposite
extreme of excessive abasement.

Universal suffrage is the most
efficient school to awaken general
intelligence, to teach a people their
rights, and to arouse in their bosoms
the sense of their manhood. For
what is a vote? It is the recognition of man's intelligence and liberty and responsibility, the qualities which constitute his manhood.
What is a vote? It is the admis-
sion that man, as man, is, or ought
to be, considered a factor in a
tolerably perfect political society;
that he has the right to shape, and
in bounden duty ought to shape
so far as his ability extends, the
course of the destiny of his country. A vote is a practical means
by which every man can exercise
his right and fulfil his duty by making his voice heard in the councils
of the nation. It is the practical
application of the truth that "all
men are born equal"—that is, "all
men have an equal right to life,"
to "liberty," and to the "pursuit of
happiness," and, armed with a bal-
lot, a man has the power of maintaining and protecting these rights.
Every vote rightly understood
means at least all that has been
here stated. The force of these
truths, by virtue of their application, effaced from the minds of the
offspring of the Puritans in less than
two generations the "injurious im-
positions of their early catechetical
instructions." It is speaking within the boundaries of moderation to
say that scarcely one descendant
of the Puritans in fifty, perhaps not
one in five hundred—shall we say
one in a thousand? perhaps not one
in ten thousand—will be found who

would willingly make, without seri-
ous reservations, an act of faith in
the five points of Calvinism. So
thorough has been this reaction
that a good part of the New England people now hold that to be
Christianity which their forefathers
would have condemned as the total
negation of Christianity. This is
not to be wondered at when you
consider that every time a freeman
goes to the polls and deposits his
vote in the ballot-box he virtually
condemns the dogmas of Protestantism and practically repudiates
the Reformation. The persistent
action of the ballot-box of the republic outweighed the persuasive
force of the Puritan pulpit.

A writer in an English periodi-
cal, commenting on this religious
phase of the New England mind
resulting from their rejection of
the doctrine of "total depravity,"
remarks: "It is now a part of the
Boston creed that a man born in
that city has no need to be born
again."

The people may not draw
promptly the conclusions which
flow from their premises, for they
act rather from implicit than explicit reflections; but in the long
run they reach the explicit logical conclusion from these premises. The early Puritans, in conforming their politics to their religion,
founded a theocracy; their descendants, in conforming their religion
to their political principles, founded Unitarianism. "I trust," wrote
Mr. Jefferson in 1822, "there is
not a young man now born in the
United States who will not die an
Unitarian." *

This truth, then, if we mistake
not, has been clearly shown: that
every religious dogma has a special
bearing on political society, and this

* Parton's *Life of Jefferson*, p. 711.

bearing is what constitutes its political principle; and every political principle has a religious bearing, and this bearing involves a religious dogma which is its premise. And, as a corollary from the above, it may be rightly said that Protestant religious dogmas are foreign to republicanism and lead to a theocracy in politics; and that republicanism in politics is foreign to Protestantism and leads to Unitarianism in religion. But Unitarianism is naturalism, and no close observer of the current of religious thought of the American people will deny that under the genius of republicanism its main drift is in that direction.

This much being said, the way is now clear to treat more satisfactorily of the relation between the republic and the Catholic Church.

There exists a necessary bond and correlation between the truths contained in the Declaration of Independence and the revealed truths of Christianity, since the truths of the natural order serve as indispensable supports to the body of revealed truths of faith. Deny to man reason, and religion can have no more meaning to men than to a brute or a machine. Deny the certitude of reason, and there would be no foundation for certitude in supernatural faith. Deny the innate freedom of the will, and the basis for all morality would be undermined, and the fountain-head of personal, political, and religious liberty would be dried up. Deny to man the gifts of reason and free-will, and the natural rights of man which flow from these gifts are the wild fancies of a dreamer, and a republic founded upon them becomes the baseless fabric of a vision.

The following declarations will throw more light on the value of human nature, and of the bearing of the truths of reason upon the supernatural truths of faith, and make our road still easier. Reason is the organ of truth, and acts upon the truth which lies within its domain with infallible certitude. The action of reason precedes faith, and can admit the claims of no authority which does not appeal with entire trust to its jurisdiction for its verification, and can accept of none that does not accord and blend with its dictates. Man is by nature in possession of his free-will; therefore freedom is a birthright, and he holds it in trust from his Creator and is responsible for its right use. Human nature, as it now exists, is essentially good, and man naturally seeks and desires his Creator as the source of his happiness. Man has lost none of his original faculties and has forfeited none of his natural rights by Adam's fall, and therefore is by nature in possession of his natural rights, and it is rightly said: "Among these are life, liberty, and the pursuit of happiness." "God has created all men equal" in regard to these rights, and therefore no one man has the natural right to govern another man; and all political authority in individuals is justly said to be derived from the consent of the collective people who are governed. The people, under God, associated in a body politic, are the source of the sovereign political power in the civil state. The light of reason is the light of God in the soul, and the natural rights of man are conferred by God directly upon man; and therefore a religion which does not affirm the value of human reason and defend the natural rights of man is baseless, and by no manner of means revealed by his Creator, but is a delusion or an imposition and worthy of no respect. With the light of these statements, the truths of which are in conformity with her authoritative teaching, the connection of the Catholic Church with the American republic can easily be understood, and at the same time the light which they shed lays bare to the view of all men the real motives which actuate Catholics in their devotion to popular rights, and places above all suspicion the sincerity of their love for popular institutions.

The American people in the Declaration of Independence avowed unequivocally their belief in the value of human nature, made a solemn act of loyalty to human reason, grounded their popular government on a solid foundation, and opened the door which leads directly to the truth. These truths which it asserted were not the fruits of philosophical speculations, but evident truths of human reason; and the rights which it affirmed were not the declamations of political dreamers, but rights inseparable from man's rational nature. Nor were these truths and these rights proclaimed to the world for the first time on the 4th of July, 1776, by the Continental Congress of the colonies; for they are as old as human nature, and will be found among the traditions of all races of civilized men. They are not lifeless abstractions but living truths, concreted more or less in all political governments, in their institutions and laws. Freedom is no tender sapling, but a hardy tree and of slow growth, whose roots are grounded in and entwined around the very elements of human nature, and under the shelter of its stout branches man has reached, through many struggles, his existing state of manhood.

The War of Independence was a struggle for man's sacred rights and liberties, and in support of these rights and liberties the colonists, as British subjects, cited the Magna Charta outlined by Cardinal Langton and his compeers, and won by them from King John in the meadow of Runnymede. Upon these inherent and acknowledged rights of man, and upon the conclusion which they derived from them that no taxation without representation ought to be permitted, as a practical maxim of government and safeguard of these rights which they had received as a legacy from our common Catholic ancestors, the war for independence began, was fought, was won; the republic was erected, and stands unchanged and immovable. Had the far-seeing Count de Maistre been as well acquainted with the history of the American colonies as he was with the history of his own country or that of England, he would not have hazarded the statement, advanced in his *Considerations on France*, that " he did not believe that the United States would last " or that "the city of Washington would accomplish the object for which it was projected." All the conditions which he considered as essential to form a nation, and the vital principles necessary to produce a constitution, were existing and gave birth to the republic. The republic came forth from these into existence as naturally as the flower expands from the bud. The illustrious count's unbelief was in contradiction to his own political doctrines no less than to the truths of his Catholic faith. He whose intellectual vision is open to the light of first principles and their main bearings, and is not altogether a stranger to true history, knows full well that the Catholic Church has battled her whole lifetime for those rights of man and that liberty which confer the greatest glory on the American republic.

That the pages of history testify to the close relationship existing between popular governments and the Catholic faith is shown by the fact that all republics since the Christian era have sprung into existence under the influence of the Catholic Church, were founded in the ages of faith and by a Catholic people. The republic of San Marino has existed in an entirely Catholic population in the heart of Italy one thousand years or more; and that of Andorra, on the borders of Spain and France, has stood the same number of years, and neither shows any signs of approaching dissolution. But these republics are small in numbers and in extent of territory? Grant it; yet they are large enough and have existed long enough to illustrate the principle that republicanism is congenial with the Catholic religion and at home in a Catholic population. Then, again, we have the Italian republics in Catholic ages—those of Venice, Pisa, Genoa, Milan, Florence, Padua, Bologna. In fact, there were no less than two hundred republics spread over the fair land of Italy. The principal Italian cities may be regarded as model republics. Some were founded in the ninth, others in the tenth or eleventh, century, and lasted several hundred years. Venice stood one thousand years and more. The Swiss republic was founded in mediæval times, and counts among its heroes and martyrs of political liberty William Tell, Arnold von Winkelried, and Andrew Hofer, all faithful sons of the Catholic Church. The republics in South America, though rather quarrelsome, are at least the growth of a population altogether Catholic. How else can we explain that the love of liberty and popular institutions should spring up spontaneously and exclusively on Catholic soil, unless it be that republicanism and the Catholic Church have one common root?

From this point of view it is a matter of no surprise that Catholics were the first to proclaim religious freedom among the original colonists, and were also among the first and stanchest patriots in the war for independence. None will be found among the signers of the Declaration of Independence whose position in society and wealth were equal to those of Charles Carroll, the intelligent, sincere, and fervent Catholic layman. The priest who became the first bishop and first archbishop in the hierarchy of the Catholic Church in the United States was the intimate friend of Benjamin Franklin, and, an associate with him, invited by Congress to engage the Canadians to be neutral if they were not ready to join their efforts for independence. Washington, with his characteristic impartiality, publicly acknowledged at the close of the war the patriotic part which Catholics as a class had taken in the great struggle for liberty. No one can appreciate the depth of conviction and the strength of affection of Catholics for republican institutions unless he sees, as they do, the same order of truths which serve as the foundation of his religious belief underlying, as their support, the free institutions of his country. The doctrines of the Catholic Church alone give to popular rights, and governments founded thereupon, an intellectual basis, and furnish their vital principle. What a Catholic believes as a member of the Catholic Church he believes as a citizen of the republic. His religion consecrates his political convictions, and this consecration imparts a twofold strength to his patriotism.

What a Catholic believes as a citizen of the republic he believes as a member of the Catholic Church; and as the natural supports and strengthens the supernatural, this accounts for the universally acknowledged fact that no Catholics are more sincere in their religious belief, more loyal to the authority of the church, more generous in her support, than the Catholic republican citizens of the United States. Catholicity in religion sanctions republicanism in politics, and republicanism in politics favors Catholicity in religion.

Their relationship is so intimate and vital that no attack can be made against the church which is not equally a blow against the republic. The animus of the so-called Native-American party was hostility to the Catholic Church, and its principles were in direct contradiction to the American bill of rights, and its policy was a flagrant violation of that religious, civil, and political liberty guaranteed by the Constitution of the United States.

The question of education affords another illustration. Catholics favor education, none more than they, and they take the strongest grounds against ignorance, for they look upon ignorance, when voluntary, as being frequently something worse than a misfortune; they even condemn it in many cases as

a sin. They are prepared, if thei rights be respected, to give thei children all the elementary, scien tific, and moral education of whicl they are capable, and even mor than the state will ever ask. A an evidence of their spirit and de votion to education witness thei schools, academies, and college dotted all over the land. No de nomination of Christians, no clas of American citizens, can stan(alongside of Catholics when it is : question of earnestness and self sacrifice for education. But " No, say the votaries of the common school system to Catholics; " w insist that you shall educate you children according to our specially devised state system, and that, too under compulsory force ; and, wha is more, you shall be taxed by th state for its support."

Catholics say in reply that it i no necessary part of the functio of the state to teach and educat children. The education of chi dren is rather a parental than political duty. Besides, to ascrib this function to the state is anti American ; for the genius of ou political system dictates that th state should abstain from all inter ference in matters which can b accomplished by individual enter prise or voluntary associations. I is clear that the chief aim of th advocates of the present public school system in the United State is less the desire for general diffu sion of knowledge than the advance ment of a pet theory of education and they insist upon its exclusiv adoption because they imagine tha its spirit and tendency are agains the spread and progress of th Catholic faith. Thus they subor dinate education to a sectaria prejudice. These feelings of hos tility to the Catholic Church actu late a considerable number of the advocates of this un-American system of what is claimed to be purely secular but really is infidel education, and to such a degree that they are blind to the fact that it is equally destructive to every form of the Christian faith; that it leaves, because of its practical inefficiency, thousands of children in ignorance; that it does violence to the religious convictions of a large body of citizens of the republic; that it tramples upon the sacred rights of parents, and endangers the state itself by perverting its action from its legitimate function. "Heat not a furnace so hot that it doth singe yourself" is good advice. The so-called American public-school system is a cunningly-devised scheme, under the show of zeal for popular education, for forcing the state, in violation of American principles of liberty, to impose an unjust and heavy tax on its citizens, with the intent of injuring the Catholic Church, while in the meantime it is sapping in the minds of the American youth the foundations of all religion and driving them into infidelity.

There are other questions, agitated only by an inconsiderable portion of the American people, and equally foreign to the genius and normal action of the republic. Some would change the Constitution of the United States, and, under the plea of Christianizing it, make it sectarian; while others, under the garb of liberty, would make the state at least pagan, if not atheistic. Had these partisans their way, the one would make the church the state, and the other would make the state the church. Catholics are content with the organic law of the republic as it stands, because it is as it ought to

be. They say to both leagues, "Protestant" and "Liberal": "Hands off from the palladium of American rights and freedom! Let there be an open field; there is no ground for fear that truth will be worsted in a fair encounter." "Truth," in the inspired words of Holy Writ, "is mighty above all things, and will prevail."

But we are told quite recently by a well-known and distinguished author, in a lecture on the "Future of the Republic," that "The Catholic Church exasperates common sense." Common sense? "Common sense" is the decision of unperverted reason, and its voice has been given counting nineteen centuries in favor of the Catholic Church, and this record has not been reversed. It was not common sense that dictated the ill-tempered sentence quoted; it bears the unmistakable ear-marks of the grim spirit of the old Puritans. The presence of the Catholic Church always did exasperate the Puritans, and acted upon their irritable nerves as her exorcisms act on evil spirits. Error always feels ill at ease when confronted by the opposite truth. This was so with the heathen, and in their exasperation they forced Catholic virgins into houses of infamy in the vain expectation of their fall. The times are changed and no longer suffer such an outrage, but in revenge this writer couples the holy church with "trance-mediums" and "rebel paradoxes." He says: "The Catholic Church, trance-mediums, and rebel paradoxes exasperate common sense." This utterance of the oracle of transcendentalism is a singular survival of the Puritan and heathen spirit, and as such it may be left to the investigations of students of atavism. To them also may be left the explanation of how, under their spell, an otherwise acute and polished writer witlessly commits a blunder against common sense and civility. "To what base uses we may return!" O Seer of Concord! it's your nerves, and you need physic.

> "Dull Sphinx, Jove keep thy fine wits!
> Thy sight is growing blear;
> Rue, myrrh, and cumin for the Sphinx,
> Her muddy eyes to clear."

Error forces truth to appear and become known; hence every new attack, every new agitation, and every newly invented calumny against the Catholic Church brings out into clearer light her divine character, removes prejudices from the minds of her adversaries, promotes conversion, and adds to her strength.

Let it, then, be clearly understood that what we maintain is that the common aim of all legitimate political government is the security of man's natural rights; that the American republic is most distinctly founded on this common basis; that the Catholic interpretation of Christianity emphatically sanctions its declaration of these rights, and as the natural and supernatural spring from one and the same divine source, "and God cannot deny himself, nor one truth ever contradict another,"* it follows that the republic and the Catholic Church can never in their normal action, if intelligence reigns, clash, but, by a necessary law of their existence, mutually aid, advance, and complete each other. A citizen of the American republic who understands himself is all the more loyal to the republic because he is a Catholic, and all the better Catholic because he is loyal to the republic. For the doctrines of the Catholic Church alone furnish him

* Vatican Council, De fide et ratione.

with the principles which enable him to make a synthesis between republicanism and Christianity.

We give below a table to show the gradual increase of the Catholic Church, so far as the data was attainable, from the time of the Declaration of Independence to the year 1878 inclusive. As for the number of Catholics, we have taken what may be considered an average estimate:

Year	1776	1790	1800	1810	1820	1830	1840	1850	1860	1878
Archbishops				1	1	1	1	6	7	11
Bishops		1	2	5	6	9	16	27	42	57
Dioceses		1	2	5	6	11	16	27	43	60
Apostolic Vicariates									3	8
Priests	25	34	50	70	150	232	482	1,800	2,235	5,650
Churches				80	120	230	454	1,100	2,385	5,720
Stations and chapels							358	595	1,128	1,800
Ecclesiastical institutions			2	3	3	9	13	29	30	33
Colleges							9	17	34	77
Female academies			1	3		6	47	91	212	595
Catholic population	25,000	30,000	100,000	150,000	300,000	600,000	1,500,000	3,500,000	4,500,000	7,000,000
Total population	3,000,000	3,200,000	5,300,000	7,200,000	9,600,000	13,000,000	17,000,000	23,200,000	31,500,000	40,000,000
Fractional part of whole population	1/120	1/107	1/53	1/48	1/32	1/21	1/11	1/7	1/7	1/6

The increase of Catholics in the United States has been due almost altogether to immigration; and when immigration diminishes will not her progress cease? The number of immigrants may fall short of what it has been, but still, for good reasons, it will continue to be large. Recently, on account of the financial crisis, it nearly stopped; but as this is now sensibly passing away the tide of immigration is again rising. This will continue; for the liberty which is enjoyed under popular institutions, and the material advantages which the country offers to settlers, especially in its cheap and fertile lands, are inducements that will suffice of themselves to attract large numbers to its shores. The millions of immigrants settled in the republic as their home and their country act as an attractive force to their relatives, friends, and former countrymen. The desire to escape the almost insupportable burden of military service by forced conscriptions, occasioned by frequent wars and by the dangers from rival nationalities continually looming with threatening aspect on the political horizon, will drive large numbers in the prime and vigor of manhood to a country that has no standing army to speak of, and whose geographical position renders it free from all threatening dangers to its peace. Last and not least of the causes bearing on this point are religious persecutions. These send large numbers, thanks especially to Prince Bismarck, to the land of religious toleration. For these and other causes, from Ireland, Germany, and other countries of Europe will flow a continuous stream of immigrants to the United States. And as three-fifths of Europe retain the

Catholic faith (omitting to count the promise of a greater increase from its Catholic population for which there are special reasons), the Catholic Church in the United States may rely on having, relatively at least, her share in the future immigrants.

But the increase of Catholics in the United States is not solely due to immigration; there is another cause, a moral and a potent one, which accelerates her growth. It has been noticed, by several authors who have written works on the population of the United States and on kindred subjects, that the natural increase of the foreign element of our population is much greater in proportion than that of the home-born element. This will be best seen by following the statistics of Massachusetts and Rhode Island, the former the largest State in New England and the latter the smallest, in population, and where registration reports have been carefully kept. Taking the population of American origin in these States as a class, their deaths exceed their birth-rate. Dr. Allen, of Lowell, who is an authority on this subject, speaking of Massachusetts, says: "It is very questionable whether there is much increase by numbers in the class of Americans." "Take," he observes, "the towns containing none or scarce any foreign populations, where in 1846 and 1865 not a single foreign birth is reported (there are thirty such towns in Massachusetts), and the whole number of deaths in these towns for 1864 and 1865 exceed each year the births." The registration report of Massachusetts for 1870 says: "The character of our population is undergoing a great change. Surely, and not slowly, a mixed stock of Irish, German, and Canadians is taking the place of the pure English stock which has possessed Massachusetts for more than two centuries." To pick and to choose and to reject among the truths known to be revealed by God is properly called heresy, and it is evident that such a state of mind is incompatible with either intellectual or moral rectitude, and therefore all heresy, by its very nature, leads inevitably to self-extinction with its fanatical adherents.

But there is an increase of population in the State of Massachusetts, and whence does this come? "Wherever an increase has taken place," observes the same writer, "it is found on examination to be made up largely of the foreign element, either from emigration or by great number of births. It is a fact now pretty well established that the foreign class will have, on an average, about three times as many children as an equal number of the American." In Rhode Island the census report of 1875 shows "that its native American population by parentage has increased only 12.89 per cent. in ten years past, while the foreign population by parentage has increased 80.11 per cent. in the same time. If this increase should continue at the same rate in the future, the population of Rhode Island will be in June, 1877: American 138,-195, and foreign 143,307; and in 1885, American 152,087, and foreign 222,466." "Old Massachusetts," remarks another writer on the subject, "has passed away, and a new Massachusetts is taking its place." But these comparative birth-rates apply with equal force to other Eastern States; and if things follow their actual course, and right names are applied to

things, New England presently will have to be called New Ireland.

The ratio of the Catholic population in all the New England States, compared with the non-Catholic, is considered at present to be about one-fourth. As Catholics are taught and believe that the bonds of wedlock are perpetually binding in conscience by a divine law, and the duties of parentage are sacred, they have no temptation to be freed from the restraints of the one or relieved from the duties of the other; or if such temptations arise they are quickly repressed by the influence of religious motives. Sad experience will teach statesmen that there is no other way of protecting the state from sure decay than in conforming its legislation to Christian morals as taught by the Catholic Church only. If the Catholic Church in the United States were left to the law of natural increase alone, this, it is evident, would suffice for her continuous progress relatively to the population of the country.

No vessel sails without back-water, and this is true of the bark of the church. Her counter-current has been in the number of her children who have strayed from her fold on account of the insufficiency of priests, churches, and the means for their religious instruction; and, again, the increased death-rate of the children of foreign parentage, occasioned for the most part by reason of poverty. As to the first drawback, the number of priests, churches, schools, these are in the larger settled States approaching to the needs of the faithful. The vocations to the priesthood in the most settled dioceses, we are informed, suffice for their wants. Seminaries are increasing; many of them are fine buildings, and that of the diocese of Philadelphia, if equalled anywhere in Catholic countries, is not surpassed. The recent decrease in immigration has given the church a breathing-spell, and she is putting forth her strength and coping with these difficulties, as the table in reference to these points on page 18 shows. As to the second, the relative poverty of Catholics, this, with their energy, industry, and spirit of enterprise, is rapidly disappearing. "From whatever branch of industry," says a Protestant writer,[*] "the Irish adopt they succeed in driving off native American competitors, and they are equally successful in establishing and maintaining in all departments under their control an enhanced rate of compensation. They have swept our factories almost clear of native help. They have nearly the monopoly of boot and shoe making, the most important and lucrative industry of Massachusetts. They are planting their colonies in many of the best towns and cities; and when they once get a foothold in a neighborhood there springs up forthwith a populous Hibernia. They are fast taking to themselves the lion's share of the actual earnings of productive industry. They are sending immense sums to Ireland; the rapidly-growing capitals of our savings-banks belong in very great part to them; they have very heavy deposits in the hands of their priests; and their ecclesiastical property is enormous, especially in our Western cities and on the Pacific coast, where the church (generally under Irish auspices) has anticipated other purchasers, and obtained at the outset corner-lots and other real estate yielding

[*] Andrew P. Peabody, D.D.

the most ample revenue, so that the Romish Church often holds more property than all Protestant denominations." But it is not only in branches of industry that Catholics have become prominent; there will be found among the distinguished merchants, bankers, judges, legislators, inventors, officers of the regular army, professors in colleges, literary and scientific men, members of the Catholic Church, and in all these classes Catholics are gaining, proportionately, representatives of their faith.

This prosperity and elevation have also their effect upon the material advancement of the church. The Catholic cathedrals, both as to size and style of architecture, are the most conspicuous structures in the largest cities in the United States, such as Philadelphia, Baltimore, Boston, Cincinnati, New Orleans, Buffalo, Newark, Cleveland, Pittsburgh, Albany, Rochester, Columbus, Mobile, Portland. Preparations are being made for the construction of cathedrals, or cathedrals are actually being built, in other populous cities—in Brooklyn, St. Louis, Providence, and Hartford. That of New York, which is on the point of completion, has, as becomes the metropolis of the Union, no rival in size, in costliness of material, and in architectural character on the continent of America. The wealth of the Catholic Church has more than kept pace with the increase of the country's wealth, as is shown by the following statement: "In 1850 the total property valuation of the United States, according to the census report of that year, was $7,135,780,228; in 1860 it was $16,159,616,068; in 1870 it was $30,668,518,507. That is to say, the aggregate wealth of the country increased about 125 per cent. from 1850 to 1860, and about 86 per cent. from 1860 to 1870.

" The total property valuation of the Roman Catholic Church in the United States in 1850 was $9,256,-758; in 1860 it was $26,774,119; in 1870 it was $60,985,565. That is to say, the aggregate wealth of the Catholic Church increased about 189 per cent. from 1850 to 1860, and about 128 per cent. from 1860 to 1870. While, therefore, in the first of these two decades, the wealth of the whole country gained 125 per cent., the wealth of the Catholic Church gained 189 per cent. ; and while in the second decade the wealth of the whole country gained 86 per cent., the wealth of the Catholic Church gained 128 per cent."

The Catholic Church in the republic finds her strength in relying for her material support upon the piety of the faithful, and the spirit and generosity with which all classes of her children respond to this test of the sincerity of their faith is an example which has a meaning at this moment for the whole Christian world. Socially and politically Catholics are slowly taking the rank to which their education, virtue, wealth, and numbers entitle them among the prominent forces of the republic, and the light which their religion throws upon its vital principles and its Constitution will make them conspicuous as intelligent and patriotic citizens.

The future of the United States belongs, under God, to that religion which, by its conscious possession of truth and by the indwelling Spirit of divine love, shall succeed in bringing the American people to · unity in their religious belief and action, as they are actually one in the political sense. It would be the utter despair of reason to suppose that truth cannot be known with certitude, and it is the virtual denial of God to question his readiness to fill the hearts of all men with his love. The thought that the existing wranglings in religion are to go on and increase for ever can only enter base minds and satisfy vulgar souls.

Admitting, then, all that has been said as true, it may be added that as the faith of the greater part of Catholics who come here from abroad rests on a traditional and historical basis almost exclusively; conceding that this traditional faith will be firm enough to keep its hold upon the immigrants and retain them in the fold of the church until death—granting all this, the question starts up forcibly here: But will not the Catholic faith, under the influence of republicanism, lose its hold in one or two, or at most in three, generations on their children ?

It is too obvious to admit of denial that a people born and educated under the influence of popular institutions will tend to exalt reason, and emphasize the positive instincts of human nature, and be apt to look upon the intrinsic reason of things as the only criterion of truth. It is equally clear that the Catholic Church, if she is to keep within her fold those who have received her baptism, and to captivate an intelligent and energetic people like the Americans, will have to receive their challenge and be ready to answer satisfactorily the problems of reason ; meet fully the demands of the needs of their spiritual nature ; bless and sanctify the imagination and senses and all man's God-given instincts. And while answering the most energetic and sublime intelligence at the bar of reason, she will have to know how to retain her sweet and gentle hold on the tenderest affections of the child.

This task will not be an arduous one; for, as has been shown, the authoritative teachings of the Catholic Church maintain the natural order as the basis of the supernatural, and, in the minds of many of the class of which we speak, Catholicity is still identified with Calvinism. Hence they do themselves the injustice to believe that in rejecting Calvinism they have also rejected Christianity altogether. They are not aware that the truths on which they based their rejection of Calvinism are affirmed by Catholicity. What they did in their repudiation of Calvinism—and Calvinism is nothing else but the logical basis of the dogmas of Protestantism—was only a repetition of the anathemas of the fathers of the Council of Trent, and their action at bottom was founded mainly on the same reasons. They have abjured Protestantism, and never can be led to go back to what they know to be hostile to the genius of their country, contrary to the dictates of reason, and repugnant to their holiest affections. Its promised heaven has lost for them all attractions; its hell no longer excites any fear in their bosoms; and its ministers openly confess that, as a religious system, Protestantism fails to exercise any authority over the minds, or to exert any influence on the conduct, of the majority of the American people. It demands from them a crippling of their nature and a sacrifice of its rights which, once its thraldom has been broken, nothing can restore. These minds have impeached Protestantism on Catholic grounds, and when

they have been led to see that their prejudices against Christianity will be removed, and they will be willing to complete their task.

They cannot rest content where they are, for the human mind was made by its Creator for truth, and in the absence of truth it ceases to live. When it refuses its assent to truth it is either because the truth has been travestied and made to appear as false, or because it is seen through a colored medium. For the intellect is powerless to reject the truth when seen as the truth. It is not in the search after truth, but in the tranquil possession of truth and appropriation of it by contemplation, that man finds the fullest and purest joy. Man craves to know the enigma of life, and until this is known his intelligence cannot be wholly content with the investigation of bugs, or baffled by a word which contains a sound and nothing more—the "unknowable."

Moreover, the American mind in one aspect is unlike the European, in that infidelity, scepticism, materialism, and atheism cannot find a lodgment in it for any length of time. Their minds, like the native soil of their country, have something virginal, and furnish no nourishment for these poisonous weeds, which, failing to take root, soon wither. There is a profound reason for this, and it will bear explanation. The reason may be found here: the denial of any one truth, carried out to its logical consequences, involves the denial of all truth. The so-called Reformers of the sixteenth century began by denying the supernatural origin of the divine institution of the church, and by force of logical sequence proceeded to the denial of its divine authority, and thus by progression to the denial of all supernatural truth; thence the denial descended to philosophy, to politics, to the entire natural order of truth, and finally to the denial of Him from whom proceeds all truth, ending in its logical termination—atheism The dominant intellectual tendency of Europe has, during these last three centuries, followed the law of negative sequence of error to its ultimate logical conclusion.

On the other hand, the affirmation of any one truth, logically followed out, leads to the knowledge and affirmation of all truth.. The American republic began afresh in the last century by the declaration of certain evident truths of reason. The law of its progression consists in tracing these truths out to their logical connection with all other truths, and finally coming to the knowledge of all truth, both in the natural and supernatural order, ending in the affirmation of universal truth and the union with the source of all truth—God. The dominant tendency of the American people is towards the law of the positive sequence of truth. The course of Europe was that of negation; the course of the United States was that of affirmation. The first was destructive, the second was constructive. The one was degrading, the other was elevating. That bred dissension, this created union. Europe, under the lead of the religious revolution of the sixteenth century, turned its back on Catholicity and entered upon the downward road that ends in death; the republic of the United States, in affirming man's natural rights, started in the eighteenth century with its face to Catholicity, and is in the ascending way of life to God.

From this point of view the Declaration of American Independence has a higher meaning, and it may be said to be the turning-point in history from a negation to an affirmation of truth: interpreting democracy not as a downward but as an upward movement, and placing political society anew on the road to the fulfilment of its divine destiny

(Christianity. like republicanism. has in the last analysis nothing else to rely upon for its reception and success than reason and common sense and the innate powers of human nature, graciously aided as they always are, and let it once be shown that the Catholic interpretation of Christianity is consonant with the dictates of human reason, in accordance with man's · normal feelings, favorable to the highest conceptions of man's dignity, and that it presents to his intelligence a destiny which awakens the uttermost action and devotion of all his powers, and you have opened the door to the American people for the reception of the complete evidence of the claims of the Catholic Church, and prepared the way for the universal acceptance of her divine character.)

The study of Zoroaster, Pythagoras, Brahma, Buddha, Confucius, Plato, Cicero, Aristotle, Marcus Aurelius, and other seers and sages of the human race, and the admiration excited by the wisdom and virtues of the most illustrious pagans, is a healthful exercise for such minds as have not been altogether emancipated from a creed which taught that the heathen were God-forsaken, · and insisted that their virtues should be "looked upon as so many vices." It may be said: What Plato did not know of the ancients was little worth knowing. Yet Justin the Philosopher, who was a devout student of Plato's writings and disciple of the doctrine of this prince of philoso- .phers, on his becoming a Christian said: "I abandon Plato, not that his doctrine is contrary to truth, but because it is insufficient and fragmentary." This, too, will be the final verdict of all earnest and honest seekers after truth among the ancient sages and philosophers; and if they have the courage to conquer their prejudices and the earnestness to pursue their studies and make an impartial investigation of the Christian religion in the light of the Catholic interpretation of its doctrines, their intellectual eyes will be opened to see that in Christianity are all the fragmentary truths which they found, after diligent and laborious search, scattered among the ancients, reintegrated in their general principles. For Catholicity affirms the convictions and traditions of the whole human race, and all the truths of every system of religion or philosophy are contained in her absolute synthesis. Catholicity means universal truth, after the knowledge of which all noble souls aspire naturally. One of the distinctive and essential marks of true religion is this: it grasps concretely whatever truth has been held always and everywhere and by all men. All truth is catholic.

There is a general conviction abroad that the people's share in the government of a nation ought to be enlarged. It must be admitted that the American republic has contributed not a little to form and support this conviction. But the principles of the republic are not like those of an Utopia in the air; they are fixedly rooted in the ground of reason and revealed truth. If the framers of the repub-lic set aside certain privileges and institutions inherited from pagan, barbaric, or feudal times, it was not to break with the past, but because these things were unserviceable to a people with the spirit and in the circumstances of the colonists. Besides, they were no less inharmonious with the more rational ideas of equity due to Christian influences; and by their omission the founders of the republic providentially advanced political government, at least for a people situated as the American people were.

When the nature of the American republic is better understood, and the exposition of Christianity is shaped in the light of its universal principles so as to suit the peculiarities of the American mind, the Catholic Church will not only keep her baptized American children in her fold, but will at the same time remove the prejudices existing in the minds of a large class of non-Catholics, and the dangers apprehended from the influence of republicanism will be turned into fresh evidences of the church's divine character.

To sum up : (He who does not see the hand of Divine Providence leading to the discovery of the western continent, and directing its settlement and subsequent events towards a more complete application to political society of the universal truths affirmed alike by human reason and Christianity, will fail to interpret rightly and adequately the history of the United States.) It is also true that he who sees Heaven's hand in these events, and fails to see that Christ organized a body of men to guard and teach these universal truths to mankind, with the promise of his presence to the end of the world, will fail to interpret rightly and adequately the history of the Catholic Church, and is like a man who sees the light but has his back turned to the sun. But he who sees all this will not fail to see that the republic and the Catholic Church, under the same divine guidance, are working together in the United States, forming the various races of men and nationalities into a homogeneous people, and by their united action giving a bright promise of a broader and higher development of man than has been heretofore accomplished.

www.ingramcontent.com/pod-product-compliance
Lightning Source LLC
Chambersburg PA
CBHW032033090426
42733CB00031B/1207